# MAKING
# a Book

Anthony Browne

**Anthony Browne**

# PIGGYBOOK

Anthony Browne

## Piggybook

**Piggybook**

**Anthony Browne**

**Piggybook**

**Anthony Browne**

Das Schweinebuch
. . . zum Abgewöhnen

**Anthony Browne**

**Piggybook**

**Piggybook**

# a Book

RUTH THOMSON
PHOTOGRAPHY : CHRIS FAIRCLOUGH

**FRANKLIN WATTS**
LONDON/NEW YORK/SYDNEY/TORONTO

Copyright © 1987 Franklin Watts

Franklin Watts
12a Golden Square
London W1R 4BA

Franklin Watts Australia
14 Mars Road
Lane Cove
N.S.W. 2066

ISBN: 0 86313 539 0

Design: Edward Kinsey
Editor: Chester Fisher
Illustrations: Susan Kinsey

Typesetting: Keyspools Ltd

Printed in Belgium

The publisher, author and
photographer would like to
thank Anthony Browne and the
Staff of Julia MacRae Books for
their great help and co-operation
in the preparation of this book.
Thanks are also due to Cambrian
Typesetters, Proost
International Book Production,
Bookpoint and Hatchards
Bookshop.

# CONTENTS

## HAVING AN IDEA

Every book you've ever read started as an idea. An author or an artist often suggests an idea to a publisher. Sometimes the publisher gives an idea to them.

The name you see on the book cover is usually only that of the author and the publishing firm. Books are, however, the work of many people – including editors, designers, production people, typesetters and printers. They could not be widely sold without the help of sales and marketing people, at the publisher and in bookshops.

▽ Did you know that over 4,000 new children's books are published in Britain every year?

6

This book follows the making of *Piggybook*, a picture book written and illustrated by Anthony Browne. He explains how the book started:

"I usually have several ideas at once floating around in my head. Gradually, one of them takes over and I start thinking out a series of pictures. At this stage, I don't think about words at all. Bit by bit, I work out how to fit the story line into 32 pages (the normal length for a picture book) and shorten or lengthen parts where necessary. I draw a series of rough sketches which only I can understand.

△ Anthony Browne, a full-time author and artist, has had ten books published.

"I write the words when I'm happy with the picture ideas. I then make a dummy, which is a model of the book with pencil sketches and handwritten words. I also paint a couple of finished pictures to show how I want to do the illustrations.

"I take these to show my publisher, who tells me at once whether she likes my idea. She also makes lots of useful suggestions to improve the book. Luckily, she gave me the go-ahead on this book, with one or two small changes.

▽ The artist at work in his studio. He works six days a week, ten or sometimes 14 hours a day.

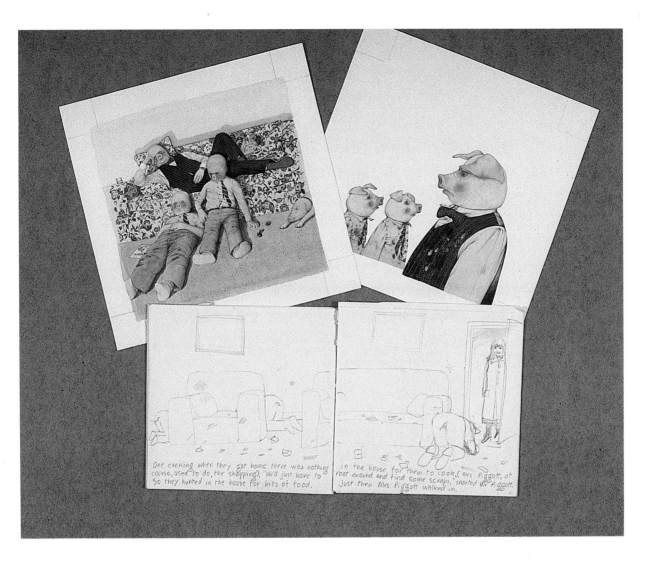

"Writing and illustrating a picture book is not always straightforward. I set to work on the illustrations but, after a while, I became unhappy about the way the pigs looked. I felt the ending of the story just wasn't right. In the end, I decided to abandon the book when I was halfway through it. I put the illustrations in a drawer and got on with other work. About two years later, I was idly looking at them again, when suddenly I thought of a much better ending. I saw a new way to draw the pigs.

△ These are the two sample illustrations and the dummy that Anthony first showed his publisher.

# THE IDEA TAKES SHAPE

"I made a new dummy and drew more illustrations which I then showed to my publisher. She liked the new ideas and wanted to publish the book as soon as possible. We decided that the book should be a larger size. This would give me room to add more details to my illustrations.

"The publisher asked the production manager to calculate the cost of the printing and to choose a printer. The production manager worked out a date by which every thing should be ready for printing.

▽ The publisher, author and production manager discuss the new dummy.

◁ The designer makes mini-designs to show how the words and pictures might fit together.

abcdefghijklmnopqrst
ABCDEFGHIJKLMN
XYZ 1234567890 12

abcdefghijklmnopqrstu
ABCDEFGHIJKLMNOP
1234567890 .,;:'"«»&!?

*abcdefghijklmnopqr*
*ABCDEFGHIJKLM*
*XYZ 1234567890 .,*

**abcdefghijklmnop**
**ABCDEFGHIJKLM**
**XYZ 1234567890**

△ Some of the many different typefaces available.

"We also discussed which typeface to use for printing the words, with a designer. There are hundreds of typefaces to choose from. The designer suggested one which would go well with my illustrations and be clear and easy to read. It was called *Plantin*.

"The designer worked out how the words and pictures would fit together. He also drew a grid which is an accurately measured drawing of a spread (two pages). The grid shows the area where the words will be put, the trim lines (where the pages will be cut) and the back (where the pages will be sewn).

▽ Typefaces can be printed in different sizes. Big type sizes are used for covers and headings.

262—8 point
ABCDEFGHIJKLMNOPQRSTUVWXYZ
abcdefghijklmnopqrstuvwxyz
1234567890 —-:;!?,.''()

262—16 point
ABCDEFGHIJKLMNO
abcdefghijkl
1234567

262—22 point
ABCDEFGHIJK
abcde
123

11

## DOING THE ILLUSTRATIONS

△ (left) The artist used his wife as a model for the mother in the book.
△ (right) The picture of the mother as it appears in the book.

"I got started on the illustrations once all those decisions had been made. I knew exactly what size and shape to make the illustrations, so that the words would fit in well with them.

"First of all, I drew a series of roughs. These are pencil sketches of the final illustrations, exactly the right size for each page. Each one provided the start of a drawing, but were quite rough and vague. A lot of my drawings come straight out of my head, but I also use things around me for reference or take photographs of things or people I want to include.

"The next stage was to trace down the roughs on to watercolour paper and paint them. At this stage, I added all sorts of extra details that I had left out or which I hadn't thought of when I was doing the roughs.

"I always start with the first page of a book and work page by page through to the last. Each one takes me about two days.

"When I had finished all the illustrations, I inked in the registration marks on the corners of the pages. These will show the designer and printer exactly how the picture is positioned on the page."

◁ The artist draws pencil roughs for each page before he paints them.

## EDITING THE BOOK

△ The editor must check the text against the illustrations.

The author's work is almost done when he delivers the manuscript and illustrations to the publishers. An editor then looks at every picture very carefully, making sure it matches with the words. The manuscript is checked for spelling, punctuation and sense.

When the editor is happy with the manuscript, it is given to the designer, who marks it ready for typesetting. The designer writes instructions to the typesetter on the manuscript. These instructions include the choice of typeface, its size and the measure (the length of each line).

# TYPESETTING THE MANUSCRIPT

The manuscript is sent to a typesetting company. Each operator has a keyboard with a VDU (Visual Display Unit). The keyboard has letters arranged in the same way as on an ordinary typewriter but also has extra keys for typographic commands.

The operator types the manuscript on the keyboard, paying attention to all the instructions which the designer has given. The operator can check on the VDU whether she has made any errors and correct them at once.

▽ The operator, at the typesetting company, looks at the VDU to check and correct her work.

△ The operator takes the galleys out of a typesetting machine.

The keyboard is connected to a typesetting machine. The operator instructs the typesetting machine to produce the typesetting in the right typeface, size and width on to special paper.

The operator sends copies of these to the editor for checking. These copies are called the galley proofs.

The editor marks corrections in two colours – those in red show mistakes made by the typesetter. Corrections in green show the changes which the editor or author want, to make the text clearer.

◁ Editors use special proof marks to make their corrections on the galley proofs.

◁ Some examples of proof correction marks.

| Marginal mark | Meaning | Corresponding mark in text |
|---|---|---|
| ꝺ⁊ | Delete (take out) | Cross through |
| ⟨ẟ⟩ / | Delete and close-up | ⌒ Above and below letters ⌣ to be taken out |
| stet | Leave as printed (when words have been crossed out by mistake) | . . . . Under letters or words to remain |
| caps | Change to capital letters | ≋ Under letters or words to be altered |
| S.C. | Change to small capitals | ═ Under letters or words to be altered |

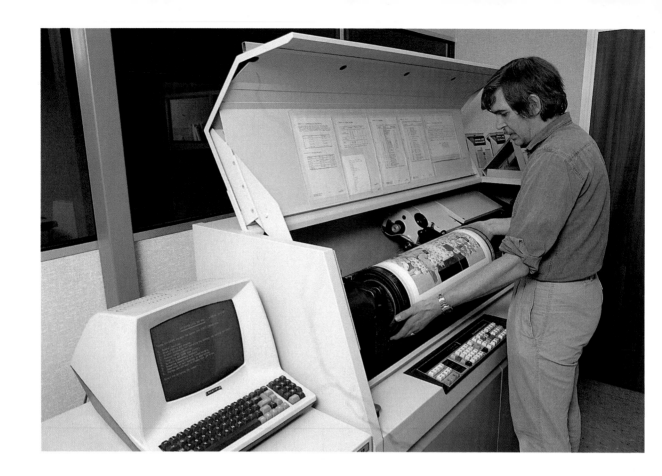

## COLOUR REPRODUCTION

△ The illustration is taped securely to the scanner cylinder.

▽ Printed colours are made up of tiny dots.

The illustrations are sent to a colour reproduction company. They make a copy of it using a special process called colour separation. If you look through a magnifying glass at a printed picture you will see that it is made up of only four colours – yellow, red (magenta), blue (cyan) and black. Every shade of colour is made by a combination of these four primary colours.

A very expensive machine called a scanner is used to reproduce colour illustrations. An illustration is taped on to the cylinder of the computer controlled scanner.

Using filters which separate the illustrations into the four primary colours, the scanner analyses the colour content of the illustration.

The computer calculates how many dots are needed to reproduce each of the colours. Separate films are produced for each of the primary colours. These are used to make proofing plates which are printed to provide colour proofs.

The proofs are carefully checked by the reproduction company and in the production department. They make sure the colours match up with the original illustration.

▷ The production staff check the colour and fitting of the proofs. They mark any corrections which need to be made to the colour film.

## THE PASTE-UP

The designer cuts up the long sheets of galley proofs and the colour proofs of the illustrations. He sticks them on layout grids in their right positions. This is called a paste-up. It shows the printer exactly how the text and illustrations should fit together.

The designer and editor then look carefully at the paste-up. They check that everything is in the right position. If all is well, the production manager sends the film of the text and illustrations to the printer with the paste-up.

▽ The editor and the designer check the position of text and illustrations on the paste-up.

△ This is how the pages will be printed. When the printed sheets are folded, each page will come out in the right place.

The printer uses the paste-up as his guide to the position of the illustration and text films. The printer cuts and arranges the film for all 32 pages in such a way that they can all be printed on one enormous sheet of paper.

The films for each colour are stuck down on separate, large sheets of clear plastic. Each sheet is put on top of a thin metal plate with a photosensitive coating.

A strong light is shone through the film on to the plate and an image of the film is etched into it.

△ ▷ The film for all four colours is positioned in the same place on each of the sheets.

# PRINTING THE BOOK

Everything is now ready for printing. Each of the four metal plates is wrapped round a cylinder and bolted into place on a huge printing press. The cylinders are well inked with either red, blue, yellow or black ink.

An enormous stack of paper is wheeled into position at the far end of the press. The press is started and some trial sheets are printed. The printer and the production manager check their colour against the colour proofs. If it is not quite right, the inking can be adjusted.

▽ The four printing inks – red, blue, yellow and black. They are very quick drying inks.

◁ The printers carefully bend the metal plate round a cylinder on the printing press.

△ The stack of paper is put into place at the end of the press.

▷ An automatic arm feeds the paper into the press.

▽ The printers and the production manager check the first sheets. When they are satisfied with the colours, the actual printing begins.

When the colour is judged to be perfect the sheets are printed, first on one side and then on the other. The image on the plate is printed on to a rubber cylinder which, in turn, prints the image on the paper as it travels through the press. The sheets are always printed in the same order of colour – first yellow, then blue, then red and lastly black. This type of printing is called offset litho.

◁ The printing press in full operation can produce up to 6,000 printed sheets per hour.

▽ How a four-colour printing press works.

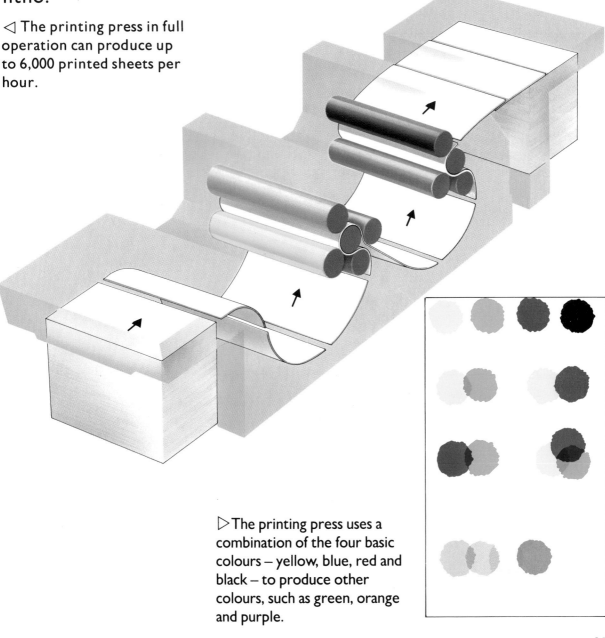

▷ The printing press uses a combination of the four basic colours – yellow, blue, red and black – to produce other colours, such as green, orange and purple.

## FOLDING AND BINDING

The printed sheets are fed, flat, into a folding machine, which first of all cuts them in half. Each half is then automatically folded several times and emerges as a section of 16 pages. Two different sections are needed for a 32 page book.

△ The printed sheets are cut and folded into 16-page sections.

▽ The sections of the book are brought together.

The sections are stitched through the centre fold. They are then trimmed to separate the pages and make them the right size for the final book. The two sections are then gathered together and glued along the spine (back).

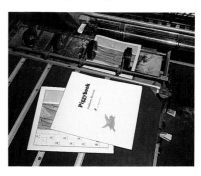

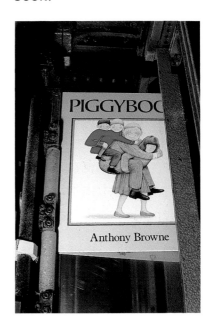

◁ The sections are fed into the binding machine.

▽ The finished case of the book.

The book covers are printed quite separately from the inside pages. Once printed, they are coated with a plastic laminate, which makes them shiny and dustproof. They are trimmed to the correct size and stacked upside down in a casemaking machine.

As each cover passes through the machine, three pieces of cardboard (a thin strip for the spine and two pieces for the sides) are glued into place. The inside pages are then glued and stitched into the finished cases. After binding, the book is complete and ready for dispatch to the publishers' warehouse.

## SELLING THE BOOK

The books at the publisher's warehouse. They are stored here while awaiting orders from bookshops and libraries.

The finished books are then stored in the publisher's warehouse to await distribution. Meanwhile, the publisher's promotion and publicity department are sending copies of the book to newspapers and magazines. The publishers hope that they will mention it and encourage people to buy the book.

The children's buyer for a large bookshop examines a finished copy of the book. The publisher's representative is hoping she will like the book and order copies for sale in the shop.

The publisher's sales representatives are visiting bookshops and library suppliers with sample copies, hoping to persuade them to order copies. The books ordered are then delivered to bookshops and libraries – ready for you to read.

# THE PROCESS AT A GLANCE

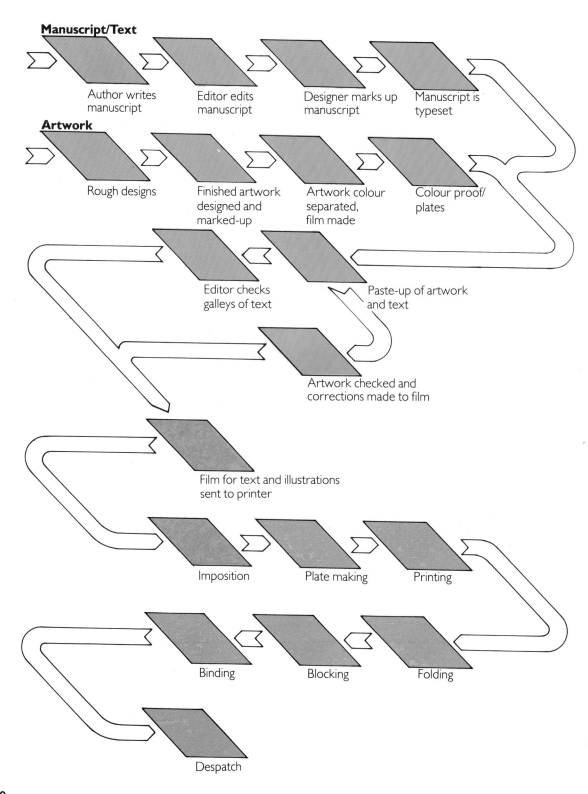

**Manuscript/Text**

Author writes manuscript

Editor edits manuscript

Designer marks up manuscript

Manuscript is typeset

**Artwork**

Rough designs

Finished artwork designed and marked-up

Artwork colour separated, film made

Colour proof/ plates

Editor checks galleys of text

Paste-up of artwork and text

Artwork checked and corrections made to film

Film for text and illustrations sent to printer

Imposition

Plate making

Printing

Binding

Blocking

Folding

Despatch

# FACTS ABOUT BOOKS

The modern book can be traced back to the Papyrus scrolls used in ancient Egypt from about 3500 B.C. These scrolls could be up to 9m (30ft) long and were unrolled as they were read. Only single copies were made.

Parchment or vellum, made from animal skins, became an important writing material in Europe from about the 2nd Century B.C. Sheets of vellum were bound between wooden boards to form the first true books.

In the Middle Ages books were very costly. Each book was the result of many months of work and the materials were very expensive. Books were usually produced by monks. Some famous books to survive are the *Book of Kells* (8th Century) and *The Winchester Bible* (12th Century).

Printing was first developed in China and Korea. In Europe the first printed book, *The Gutenberg Bible*, was produced by Johannes Gutenberg in Mainz, Germany, between 1450 and 1455.

Printing then spread rapidly throughout Europe. Printed works appeared in Italy (1453), France (1470), Hungary (1473), Spain (1473), Poland (1474), England (1476), Sweden (1483) and Mexico (1539). William Caxton was the first person to print books in English.

A power-driven printing press was first used in 1811 by the German Frederick Koening. His press raised the number of pages printed in an hour from 250 to 1,000. A rotary press invented in 1948 achieved 24,000 copies per hour. Today some machines can print up to 1 million pages per hour. Printing has become a high technology industry which uses the latest computer and laser techniques.

Over 58,000 new books were published in Britain in 1986. Of these, over 4,000 were children's books. In 1985 3,570 new Australian titles were published, of which 450 were children's books.

The world's most widely distributed book is the Bible. Parts of it have been translated into 1,763 languages. Since 1816 2,400 million copies of *The Bible* have been produced.

Over 800 million copies of *Quotations from the Works of Mao Zedong* were produced during the years 1966–9 in China.

The world's best selling book is the *Guinness Book of Records*. It was first published in 1955 and has sold over 50 million copies. *Dr Spock's Common Sense book of Baby and Child Care* has sold over 25 million copies.

In 1983 a book was sold for £8,140,000. It was a decorated manuscript called *The Gospels of Henry the Lion* which was written in Germany 800 years ago.

In 1985 the British publishing and printing industry employed a total of 41,000 people.

The total number of books sold in Britain in 1985 was estimated to be: hardback – 361 million copies, paperback – 372 million copies.

# INDEX

PRINTED IN BELGIUM BY
proost
INTERNATIONAL BOOK PRODUCTION